Creative professionalism

The role of teachers in the knowledge society

David Hargreaves

First published in
December 1998

by

Demos
9 Bridewell Place
London EC4V 6AP
Tel: 0171 353 4479
Fax: 0171 353 4481

Arguments 22

ISBN 1 898309 79 5

CONTENTS

Acknowledgments

I am much indebted David Jackson and Michael Fielding for perceptive criticisms of an early draft.

Knowledge is the only meaningful resource today.
Peter F Drucker, Post-Capitalist Society, 1993

In the industrial mode of development, the main source of productivity lies in the introduction of new energy sources ... In the new informational mode of development, the source of productivity lies in the technology of knowledge generation, information processing and symbolic communication.
Manuel Castells, The Rise of the Network Society, 1996

We need to create conditions, even inside large organizations, that make it possible for individuals to get the power to experiment, to create, to develop, to test – to innovate. Whereas short-term productivity can be affected by purely mechanical systems, innovation requires intellectual effort. And that, in turn, means people. All people. On all fronts ... people at all levels, including ordinary people at the grass roots and middle managers as the heads of departments, can contribute to solving organizational problems, at inventing new methods or pieces of strategy.
Rosabeth Moss Kanter, The Change Masters, 1983

New Labour, education policy and the teachers

The election of the new Labour government in 1997 was greeted with pleasure by many who work in the education service. Though some of the detail remained unspecified, education was to be the government's priority. It is now evident that the demands on the education service and on teachers have continued to rise. This in itself is not new. What is new is that the education policies are both conservative and radical, a combination that has puzzled and confused teachers.

The conservative aspect is exemplified in the determination to make 'the basics' an educational priority. A mastery of literacy and numeracy, especially at primary school, is the key to every child's access to the rest of the school curriculum, and so an essential right of every child in a society committed to equality of opportunity. Many have been astonished by the forcefulness of David Blunkett's speedy implementation of the national literacy and numeracy strategies, with explicit and ambitious targets for schools and local education authorities – a move which has in places been interpreted as a further and unnecessary 'top-down' imposition on over-burdened teachers. Yet the gap between those who become literate and numerate quickly and easily, and those for whom the acquisition of these skills is painstakingly slow and difficult, is unacceptably wide, for it becomes the source of under-achievement and reinforces the culture of failure that mars our educational system at secondary school and beyond. It is this spirit which lies behind the government's justifiable emphasis on homework and home–school agreements.

The radical aspect of government policy is twofold. Firstly, it is characterised by the readiness to tackle old problems with new solutions, ones not usually associated with the Labour Party. The solution to the problems of underachievement and deprivation is no longer seen to lie merely in additional resources. In the designated Education Action Zones there will be extra resources, but also new partnerships and new educational designs. And if that is to come from the private sector, so be it. Teachers can no longer assume that seriously underperforming schools and incompetent teachers and headteachers will be tolerated and protected. The tough line adopted by Chris Woodhead, the Chief Inspector at the Office for Standards in Education (OfSTED), has been endorsed by Labour to the dismay of many teachers. If closing failing schools and removing incompetent teachers and headteachers causes temporary disturbance, so be it. One difference between old Labour and new Labour is this rejection of the belief that educational problems are mostly soluble by palatable methods, usually an increase in resources. It is a tenet of new Labour that to solve old problems new ways must be devised and implemented.

Secondly, there is a strong response to emerging challenges. The huge spending on laying down the infrastructure for the information and communication technologies (ICT) and their growing role in education is the best example. There is clearly a eye on 'the school of the future' as well as the potential of ICT to raise levels of achievement in the schools of today. The publication of a Green Paper on the future of the teaching profession reveals the government's recognition that teachers are the key to revitalising the education service and to bridging the gap between the school of today and the school of future.

This pamphlet argues that the agenda of educational renewal now needs to become yet more radical. Transforming our educational system requires solutions to some new problems which, if left unrecognised and unattended, will overwhelm teachers and undermine the achievement that accompanies higher levels of numeracy and literacy in primary schools and rising performance in public examinations at secondary level. The drivers of educational change are not always those of governmental policy; rather, it is rapid and continual change in the wider society that makes an impact on education. Government can help by reconceptualising the role and professional identity of teachers and by providing conditions under which they can adapt successfully to these changes. The quality of education always hinges on effective teaching and learning. As the pace of change is high, teachers must now be helped to *create* the professional knowledge that is needed.

The recruitment and retention of high quality teachers is a prerequisite of raising standards. Teaching, I argue, must become a profession in which able graduates believe they can play innovative roles in the task of professional and institutional reshaping that is required with the emergence of 'the knowledge society'. Until teaching is perceived, *inter alia*, as a profession in which creative and adventurous but hard-headed pioneers feel at home, the negative image of the profession will persist. Without teachers of the highest quality, the chance of meeting the challenges presented by the knowledge society will swiftly decline.

So what are these new problems that must soon be solved? Some arise from changes in family, household and community structures and changing moral and religious beliefs and commitments. It is left to schools to take an increasingly active role in preparing the young to be decent members of society – to learn how to distinguish right from wrong, to acquire the virtues of active citizens in a democratic society and to prepare to be good parents and neighbours. Neither the traditional curriculum, in which citizenship and many aspects of moral education are marginal, nor the conventional ways in which schools are linked to their partners – parents, employers, community organisations – are adequate to help teachers to cope with these new responsibilities.

Other problems arise from the changing nature of work. Many fields of employment require competence and confidence with ICT, and so today another 'basic' must be added to the school curriculum: information technology skills, in which most teachers are inadequately versed. Moreover, the conventional lifelong career – which is the life pattern of so many teachers – is in decline. Many young people will enter employment on the assumption of pursuing multiple careers requiring lifelong learning. As many jobs will effectively disappear after a few years, people will have to learn how to 'redesign' themselves: examine the job market for opportunities, decide what skills and qualifications are needed, and then seek out the education and training required. In the knowledge society, employability involves qualities of flexibility, creativity, entrepreneurship and networking. Future workers will need to be self-managers rather than managed employees, team players rather than individual stars. Many teachers are familiar with, and fascinated by, the writings of Charles Handy, Peter Drucker and Charles Leadbeater but find it hard to work out how schools and teachers need to change to prepare young people for this new world.

Young people learn most readily from those they want to be like. Many boys learn quickly from coaching by professional footballers because they want to be like them. The trouble with teachers is that their students do not want to be like them. Ways must be found to enable teachers to enact and exemplify, not just talk about, the very qualities required to be successful in the knowledge society. In the same way, the ethos and life of the school imbues students with notions of what a community is and how it provides a way of life. It is pointless for teachers to preach about a future community that is belied by the structure and character of the community that currently exists in school. Teachers help the young to appreciate their cultural heritage; they must now also prepare them for a world in which some new skills are at a premium.

So teachers and schools must stop serving as role models of fading career structures and moribund communities and begin to model people who are team-playing, networking and community-supporting, with an ability to be continually creative in a world in which, by definition, fresh problems unfold but must be solved *quickly and locally*. This is the way to cultivate in students the personal, moral and communal qualities that will matter in, and so be a preparation for, the knowledge society. To play their full part, teachers must help to shape the education system of the future rather than simply functioning within it. This is the vision of post-millennial teachers.

The argument

Designing better schools and training better teachers for the knowledge society is a gigantic task, one that involves finding new ways of discovering 'what works' in schools and classrooms. And this process of knowledge creation and application must be a continuous one, since society continues to change very fast, constantly making new demands on the education service. The argument of this pamphlet is that today's dominant models for *creating, disseminating and applying* professional knowledge for teachers are now

- almost entirely inappropriate and ineffective
- a serious waste of material and human resources
- adding to the low morale and the serious shortage of teachers.

The answer, I argue, lies in a new model of knowledge creation, one based on evidence of success in other sectors of society. To be effective in education, this new model must be adapted to support the continuous development and self-renewal of better teachers and teaching. This means:

- rethinking the role of practising teachers in the creation, application and dissemination of professional knowledge about what works in schools and classrooms
- reconstructing the relationships between universities, the seat of most teacher training and educational research, and the schools, whose needs they ostensibly serve
- aligning the relations between researchers and practising teachers with those between researchers and engineers in highly successful, knowledge-intensive firms
- developing new conceptions of school effectiveness, school improvement and professional development to meet the demands of the knowledge society
- turning teaching into a job with far more opportunities for teachers to be creative in ways that mirror the style of suc-

cessful practitioners in other professions
- persuading government to devise policies to shape the attitudes and actions needed to ease the transition of the education service into the knowledge society.

Without this, the government will be unable to renew and re-motivate the profession to adapt to changing demands and priorities, and the teachers will lack the self-confidence, energy and creativity to realise the full potential of the education service to raise standards.

How we are failing to meet the challenge

To some, the scale of social change envisaged in the knowledge society is being grossly exaggerated and so radical changes in the education service are not necessary. There is a belief that there are more familiar and less risky ways of responding to whatever challenges may lie ahead. More generous funding for educational research in universities and for disseminating the outcomes to schools will, it is said, spearhead the desired improvements. In a related approach, it is held that much professional 'good practice' already exists in schools, and an improved capacity to spread it from outstanding schools to the rest is what is now needed. Are these beliefs justified?

Educational research to the rescue?
In this country, £65 million is spent each year on educational research, almost all of it by researchers employed in higher education, usually teacher training. Much of this research has been widely criticised – for its poor quality, its irrelevance to educational policy and its inapplicability to the improvement of what happens in schools. In the summer of 1998, this diagnosis was confirmed by an independent review of educational research commissioned by the Department for Education and Employment. There is good educational research, some of a fundamental kind and some that is applicable to policy and practice, but there is far too little of it. Researchers insist that their work is relevant to teachers, but – as we shall see – relevance is no longer enough.

Part of the explanation for this sorry state of affairs is that it is researchers who decide how to spend the research funds; policymakers and practitioners are hardly involved in deciding what shall be researched or how that research shall be evaluated. Researchers form an exclusive club in which an elite decides which members shall have the money to do what. Rightly, some of the funding is allocated to topics and ideas that have no short-term application: these are sensible investments in the medium to long-term. But too much educational research is destined never to be applicable to, or have any serious bearing on, any policy or practice: it has become an academic self-indulgence. Something has gone seriously wrong with educational research. A start is being made on addressing the faults, but reform must be radical if research is to provide teachers and policy-makers with the help they now need.

Better dissemination of 'good practice'?

Another approach is to acknowledge that some highly effective teaching and learning – usually called 'good practice' – already occurs in the most successful schools. If, it is said, this could only be disseminated to every school, the quality of teaching and learning would rise sharply. On the basis of inspections, OfSTED is now identifying such schools, which are given money to act as 'beacon schools' spreading good practice to others. The difficulty here is that surprisingly little is known about effective ways of disseminating within education systems, either from universities to schools or from one school to another. The evidence is that such dissemination is complicated and rarely successful. Conventional methods of dissemination, through books, articles in journals, government pamphlets, videos, even courses for teachers, have an alarmingly poor record of changing what goes on in classrooms.

Untrustworthy forms of dissemination are still in constant use. It may be because this diverts blame for poor implementation from the disseminator ('I play my part by informing you about research findings or good practice...') to the teacher ('...but you don't respond as you're supposed to'). It may be because the disseminators don't see any alternative. It is time to accept that traditional models of dissemination are discredited, have severe limitations and can't be made to work by spending more on them or by patching them up. Something better has to be devised.

Two conditions of effective dissemination

Methods of dissemination will be successful in meeting the educational challenge under two conditions. First of all, we must uncover the normal conditions under which teachers naturally change their practices and then use the methods of dissemination – beacon schools, books and videos, and in-service courses – to support this. Traditional dissemination often fails because it runs against the grain of how teachers do their work and manage the process of change. As Michael Huberman (1992) has observed:

> Essentially teachers are artisans working primarily alone, with a variety of new and cobbled together materials, in a personally designed work environment. They gradually develop a repertoire of instructional skills and strategies, corresponding to a progressively denser, more differentiated and well integrated set of mental schemata; they come to read the instructional situation better and faster, and to respond with a greater variety of tools. They develop this repertoire through a somewhat haphazard process of trial and error, usually when one or other segment of the repertoire does not work repeatedly.... When things go well, when the routines work smoothly ... there is a rush of craft pride.... When things do not go well ... cycles of experimentation ... are intensified.... Teachers spontaneously go about tinkering with their classrooms.

Teachers do not uncritically accept drastic changes to their work when these are suggested from outside; their reaction is one of sceptical caution. Teachers have learned to trust other teachers, rather than researchers or government ministers, about 'what works' in classrooms, and even then they need to 'tinker' with an idea to see how well it fits their personal style and the conditions of their particular classroom.

Secondly, it has to be recognised that even the best schools do not possess the solutions to the emergent problems discussed above. Consider what have been shown to be the characteristics of the most effective schools (Sammons *et al*, 1995):

- professional leadership

- shared vision and goals
- a learning environment
- concentration on teaching and learning
- purposeful teaching
- high expectations
- positive reinforcement
- monitoring progress
- pupil rights and responsibilities
- home–school partnership
- a learning organisation.

None of this is surprising, but there are reservations. This list derives from common-sense measures of features taken to be relevant in schools judged to be effective. Other teacher practices might prove to be important in raising pupil achievements if only they had been measured. For example, it seems that formative feedback is more valuable to student learning than praise from teachers. Moreover, knowing the characteristics of the most effective school does not tell us how to make less effective schools become like the best. Even more worryingly, this is a retrospective picture of effective schools now, but we cannot be sure that today's effective schools will meet the challenges for schools that arise in the knowledge society. The only hint of a forward look is in the last feature – the school as 'a learning organisation' – but the idea is vague and undeveloped. How tomorrow's schools and teachers will learn to find solutions to new problems is not specified.

Meeting the challenge: new professional knowledge

A prerequisite of the way forward is to work with the grain of the psychology and experience of teachers by ensuring that they themselves actively contribute to better professional practices. Teachers, like doctors or engineers, naturally 'tinker' to discover 'what works best' and in so doing they creatively search for, and test out, the solutions to the problems. The task is to find, on a grand scale, a new way in which teachers can create the professional knowledge (which includes the associated practical skills) they need, devise ways of testing whether this know-how works and then find effective and efficient ways of disseminating the outcomes.

Headteachers and teachers, like all professionals, possess a *working knowledge* that enables them to carry out their job well. At the heart of better teaching, then, is the need to improve teachers' professional working knowledge in five key aspects:

- *Working knowledge of how to manage the school*
  Leadership from the headteacher is known to be a key feature of effective schools. Nothing canvassed in this pamphlet is achievable without heads who have sound knowledge of how to manage the school – and especially its major asset, the teachers.
- *Working knowledge of how to manage teaching and learning*
  Some of this is knowledge of the curriculum subject being taught. Knowing one's subject is a necessary but not sufficient condition for being a good teacher. For this, the art of teaching in such a way that student learning occurs is also necessary. Here is the principal focus of projects to improve schools.
- *Working knowledge of how to manage the school's external partnerships*
  This, an old problem, becomes ever more important. It has been known for decades that where teachers treat parents as

co-educators, the students' motivation and achievements are greatly enhanced. The record of schools in maximising the benefits of home–school partnership is patchy and generally poor. Yet in the knowledge society, schools will need to manage many more partnerships – with the world of work, with many other agencies concerned with informal as well as formal education, including the media of digital radio and television and a new partnership between teachers and commercial developers of educational software to exploit to the full potential of ICT for schools. This means teachers working with other adults as educational partners, but teachers have been trained to work with children, not adults. The school can no longer work in isolation if it wants to succeed. Managing collaborative partnerships is crucial. Teachers will need considerable help and support to forge this new professional working knowledge.

- *Managing the creation of new working knowledge for teachers and heads*
- *Managing the dissemination of this new knowledge to every single school.*

These last two are the critical and central concerns of this pamphlet.

A lesson from science and technology

In science and technology, the successful production of useful knowledge has undergone a profound change. Two kinds of knowledge creation have been distinguished, labelled Mode 1 and Mode 2 (Gibbons, *et al*, 1994). Expressed concisely, Mode 1 is university-based, pure, disciplinary, homogeneous, expert-led, supply-driven, hierarchical, peer-reviewed. Out of Mode 1 evolves Mode 2, in which knowledge production is applied, problem-focused, trans-disciplinary, hybrid, demand-driven, entrepreneurial and embedded in networks.

Because Mode 1 is the dominant form and associated with the universities, it is more easily understood and recognised. Mode 2 is strongly concerned with knowledge that is useful – to a policy maker or a 'user' – and is not created at all until various groups negotiate its production, usually from different types of knowledge. Mode 2 knowledge is not created in a university by researchers and then applied somewhere in the real world by practising professionals: it evolves within the context of its application out in the real world, but then may not fit neatly into Mode 1 knowledge structures. The team generating the knowledge may consist of people of very different backgrounds working together temporarily to solve a problem. The number of sites where such knowledge can be generated is greatly increased; they are linked by functioning networks of communication. The knowledge is then most readily diffused, not so much through books or academic journals, but through informal and personal channels, as when those who participated in its original production move to new situations. Individual creativity is the driving force of Mode 1 knowledge; in Mode 2, creativity is generated in and by the group, which may nevertheless contain members socialised in Mode 1 forms.

In other words, Mode 1 is university-centred knowledge creation; Mode 2 is knowledge creation through applied partnerships. It is evident that most of the knowledge produced by educational researchers in universities and subsequently disseminated to teachers in schools is Mode 1 research, with a sharp boundary between knowledge production and utilisation. Parts of educational research are making a transition to Mode 2 knowledge production, and this is a desirable shift. But while some Mode 1 'basic' research in education should be protected, the pace and scale of the transition to Mode 2 must increase dramatically if government targets for educational improvement are to be met. This would herald a major and largely unwelcome change for education researchers.

The creation of high quality knowledge about effective teaching and learning that is actionable in classrooms requires practising teachers to share the process with researchers who are closer to them. It will be painful for the academics to lose their high control over educational research. Some researchers have been questioning and progressively abandoning the 'linear model' by which knowledge is created by researchers, then disseminated and supposedly applied by teachers to their practice. Neither researchers nor government departments and agencies have taken the implications of the failure of the linear model to the obvious conclusion that knowledge creation and dissemination in education must now move into Mode 2: teacher-centred knowledge creation through partnerships.

Such Mode 2 type operations already flourish in business and industry:

[W]hilst often drawing extensively on external sources like universities and government labs, in most industries the lion's share of innovative effort is made by the firms themselves. There are several reasons for this. First, after technology has been around for a period of time, in order to orient innovative work fruitfully one needs detailed knowledge of its strengths and weaknesses and areas where improvement would yield high payoffs, and this knowledge tends to reside with those who use the technology, generally firms and their customers and suppliers.... Where universities or public laboratories do seem to be helping national firms, one tends to see either direct interactions between particular firms and particular faculty members or research teams, as through consulting arrangements, or mechanisms that tie university programmes to groups of firms.... In all of these cases, the relationships between the university ... and industry are not appropriately described as the universities ... simply doing research of relevance to the industry in question. The connections were much broader and closer than that, involving information dissemination and problem solving. Universities and industry were co-partners in a technological community. (Nelson, 1996)

A lesson from business and industry

Schools, the objection runs, are very different from commercial companies. So why look at business and industry? Because it is here, as the distinction between Modes 1 and 2 suggests, that helpful clues to the specification of 'knowledge-creating schools' may be discerned. In parts of business *creating and applying* new knowledge is the only way to survive commercially. In 'high technology' and electronics firms of computers, micro-processors, semi-conductors and so on, knowledge moves very fast indeed, so the creation and application of new knowledge are an organisational priority. Such firms understand that to be content with current knowledge and practice is to be left behind. The penalty for failing to create the knowledge is severe. Knowledge can very quickly become redundant; practices that once worked have to be abandoned and replaced. Moreover, these firms recognise that their principal assets are not financial and material, but human – the people who work for and with them. Effective use of *intellectual capital* is vital to knowledge-intensive companies. Are not schools in a very similar position? Is there a lesson to be learned?

A study of the literature indicates that successful electronics companies that have created and exploited new knowledge – knowledge-intensive firms such as Hewlett-Packard, Intel, Motorola and Texas Instruments – have distinctive characteristics. I have examined the research on organisational effectiveness in industrial knowledge creation – of which more later – and from this I generate a picture of how it might be applied to educational organisations and systems. There is, not surprisingly, a close fit with how a Mode 2 education service might look. On this theoretical basis, knowledge-creating schools would display four clusters of characteristics.

1. The first is a *new openness to the outside world beyond the classroom*, including:
    - a strong awareness of the external environment, including

opportunities and pressures, and a capacity to recognise, assimilate and exploit external knowledge

- sensitivity to the expectations and preferences of students, parents and governors.

2. As a result, the culture of the school and its organisational structures are modified, as exemplified in:

- a culture of, a commitment to and an enthusiasm for continual improvement
- institutional planning that is coherent (producing a shared organisational state of mind and a clear strategic framework) but flexible (allowing an opportunistic response to events)
- decentralisation and flat hierarchies, groups being given the responsibility for scrutinizing ideas and decision-making within their sphere of action
- internal hybridisation, that is, cross-functional teams and job rotation
- temporary developmental structures outside the bureaucratic maintenance structures – task forces of people who come together to solve a problem and disband after completing the task
- a positive climate with a constant and explicitly maintained tension between liberty and control, freedom and responsibility in professional work.

3. Within this framework, new kinds and styles of relationship emerge, with a focus on:

- informality of relationships among staff who value task-relevant expertise rather than organisational status and engage in high volumes of professional talk through intensive internal networking – 'knowledge sharing, not knowledge, is power'
- a recognition by managers of the specialised, expert knowledge held by teachers
- encouragement of diversity, deviant ideas being a poten-

tial seedbed of innovation
- the provision of regular opportunities for reflection, dialogue, enquiry and networking in relation to professional knowledge and practice, and a high commitment to continuing professional development.

4. Most important of all, knowledge creation becomes a central activity of teachers:
   - professional knowledge creation is not seen as the chance quirkiness of a minority of 'creative' individuals, but as a whole-school process that has to be managed
   - a readiness to tinker and experiment in an ad hoc way with new ideas, or variations on old ideas, is encouraged and supported, in order to do things better, within a culture that does not blame individuals when things prove not to be good enough, mistakes being treated as paths to learning
   - teachers become ready to engage in alliances and networks to further such work, including networking with other schools: since no school can alone create all the knowledge needed, sharing is essential and in the interests of all.

Some schools are well on the way to developing these features, which are by no means the same as the characteristics of effective schools listed earlier. In my view this new list, adapted from business, is a more insightful and suggestive description of the successful school in the knowledge society.

The making of a knowledge-creating school

Based on what we know about knowledge-creating organisations in other areas, the knowledge creating school:

- investigates the state of its intellectual capital
- manages the process of creating new professional knowledge
- validates the professional knowledge created
- disseminates the created professional knowledge.

Let us explore each of these.

Investigating a school's intellectual capital

How much professional knowledge is there in a school? The question is not usually asked. Let us imagine a moderately large secondary school with 45 teachers, and put the following questions to them.

- *How many years of professional experience are there among the teaching staff of your school?*
- *How much of this professional knowledge is:*
  - *shared by all the teachers?*
  - *shared by some of the teachers?*
  - *locked in the heads of individual teachers?*

The typical answer to the first question is between four and five centuries. The answer to the second is that most of it is locked in the heads of individuals and not accessible to other teachers. Schools make poor use of their collective professional knowledge.

A school's teachers need to find out what they know, not least because they know more than they think. They also need to know what they do not know – for that is the area where they must create better professional knowledge. To do this means bringing to light knowledge they did not realise they possessed – knowledge which may be held by one or two teachers but nobody realises

Figure 1. Investigating knowledge and ignorance

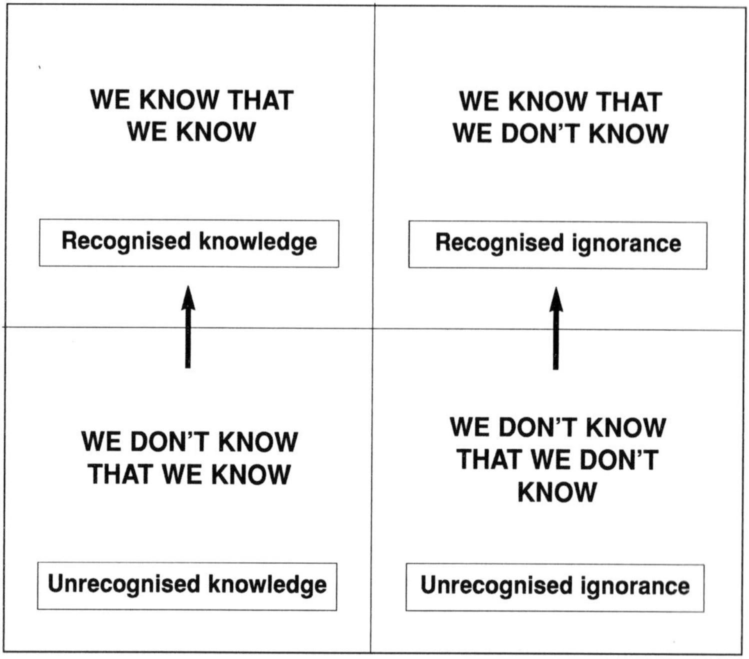

WE KNOW THAT WE KNOW	WE KNOW THAT WE DON'T KNOW
Recognised knowledge	Recognised ignorance
↑	↑
WE DON'T KNOW THAT WE KNOW	WE DON'T KNOW THAT WE DON'T KNOW
Unrecognised knowledge	Unrecognised ignorance

this – and acknowledging that they are collectively ignorant of knowledge they thought they possessed (see Figure 1).

A school cannot be a 'learning organisation' if it is unaware of what it knows and does not know. Each teacher has a professional knowledge base. There is a complex social distribution of professional knowledge within a school. When exposed by the investigation, planned and coordinated action on the sharing of existing professional knowledge can be undertaken to provide an organisational knowledge base and to give direction to the creation of new knowledge. A school might select an area for knowledge mapping by doing a survey with questions such as:

● *Which colleague has helped you improve an aspect of your teaching in what ways?*
● *What do you do in your classroom that others might find use-*

ful or interesting?

- *What aspects of your own teaching do you think you're best at?*

The results can be used to inform all the staff about whom to contact if one wants help and advice or an opportunity to talk about a particular classroom issue.

For school leaders, the management of professional knowledge creation requires a grasp not only of the capital embedded in individuals and groups among the staff, but also among the students, their families and local communities. No enquiry into a school's intellectual capital is complete unless the knowledge of all the school's members and partners is recognised. Teachers do not always need to create the knowledge they need: they need to know who among their partners already has it and how to access it.

Managing the creation of new professional knowledge

Part of a school's intellectual capital is the 'managerial capital' owned by the headteacher and senior staff – the professional knowledge and skill of how to manage the school. One of the most important pieces of managerial capital is *knowledge of how to manage knowledge creation*. Our current understanding of this is limited, but may be expressed as five steps – each of which can be linked to the horticultural metaphor beloved of educationalists since Plato.

Step 1. Generating ideas: sowing

This requires, above all, a school culture which holds that all teachers are potentially creative in what they do and which promotes tinkering so that they actively try out new ideas or adapt old ones and take carefully calculated risks in so doing.

Some of the professional knowledge of teachers is *explicit*, that is, it is easily talked about or even written down. But much of the knowledge is *tacit*, that is, not easily expressed in words but

Figure 2. The Nonaka and Takeuchi model of knowledge creation

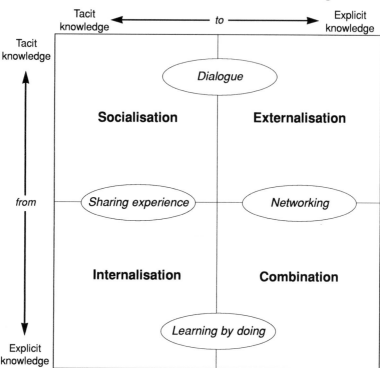

embedded in skilled action in the classroom. There are some things that are more easily done than said. Teachers make clever decisions which are right in the circumstances, but often they cannot explain to an outsider exactly *how and why* they did what they did. This kind of practical know-how is at the core of the highest quality teaching and is the richest seam in the creation of better professional knowledge.

In the best current theory of knowledge creation, that of Nonaka and Takeuchi (1995), the interaction between explicit and tacit knowledge is a key to new knowledge (see Figure 2). In the process of knowledge creation, one type of knowledge, explicit or tacit, is converted into knowledge of the same or a different kind.

Socialisation concerns the *shared experience* through apprenticeship and on-the-job training which generates and transmits tacit knowledge. *Dialogue* and collective reflection among members of the community trigger externalisation by which tacit knowledge is articulated into explicit knowledge. *Learning by doing* stimulates internalisation, by which explicit knowledge is converted into tacit knowledge; as in skill acquisition, what is initially explicit becomes tacit through experience. People with different knowledge coming together through *networking* results in combination, a process of systematising and elaborating explicit knowledge by combining different bodies of knowledge.

This ingenious theory cannot be fully explained and explored here. Its rich potential for application to education will be clear to those who study the original text. Here I show how closely the theory's key concepts relate to educational knowledge creation. In the knowledge-creating school, the headteacher establishes conditions to maximise professional talk among staff about teaching and their tinkering activities in classrooms. In this way, the key processes of sharing experience, dialogue, networking and learning by doing are activated and directed along knowledge-creating tracks. The foundations for more systematic knowledge-creation by teachers in schools are already well established.

Step 2. Supporting ideas: germinating
In a knowledge-creating school teachers generate many good ideas for development. Good ideas – especially when they come from new or more junior colleagues – are fragile and may well need protection by the most experienced teachers from colleagues inclined to intellectual infanticide. Cynics kill knowledge creation.

Step 3. Selecting the most promising ideas: thinning
Despite the abundance of good ideas, not all can be fully developed at once. Some need to be abandoned or postponed to leave enough time for those selected. The criteria for selection of the best must be clear and those whose ideas are not pursued immediately should not lose face.

Step 4. Developing ideas into knowledge and practice: shaping and pruning

Here is one of the key elements of knowledge creation, namely how the knowledge is validated or really shown to work and made robust and trustworthy. This is discussed in detail below. It must also be understood that when some new practice is validated, it should lead to the abandonment of old practices that cannot be validated. Newly created knowledge must replace invalid practice.

Step 5. Disseminating knowledge and practice: showing and exchanging

New knowledge and practices, once validated, have to be made accessible to other teachers though internal networks. The effective manager of knowledge creation creates channels by which the outcomes of creation are widely distributed, for such channels do not exist in most schools. This is also discussed in more detail below.

Validating professional practice: is 'best practice' really best?

In the literature on successful electronics firms there is little on the validation of the created knowledge, for there are three obvious validation tests: there is an explicit scientific base; 'it works' so it does not matter if the underpinning science is unclear; and 'it sells', the commercial test. In education, by contrast, the validation of professional knowledge and practice is a major issue. Here, applied knowledge is validated when it is turned into a practice which demonstrably and repeatedly works and can be used or adapted by different practitioners in a range of contexts. A practice that works only in very restricted circumstances or is not transferable to other teachers cannot be regarded as useful knowledge.

Because in educational circles professional knowledge has become disconnected from validation, there is profound confusion about

● a good idea, which may be worthwhile but has not been sub-

ject to any kind of test
- a good practice, which implies some kind of validation that it is sound, and
- best practice, which implies a (good) practice that is demonstrably better than others.

This muddle about 'good practice' and purported 'best practice' (which often has no evidential base) strikes at the very heart of any drive to raise standards and to improve the quality of teaching and learning. Since teachers in schools work for the most part on their own in a state of professional isolation, they adopt the method of trial and error to discover through personal experience what works for them. Knowledge validation is reduced to 'what works for me' – but the criteria by which a practice is judged to work remain obscure. This is patently not a way in which standards can be raised. How to validate professional practice has yet to be addressed.

Teachers sometimes *talk* to one another about their practices, but only relatively rarely do they *watch* one another at work or even practise together with a self-conscious attempt to validate a practice – what we might call 'trial-and-improve tinkering'. Such *social* validation is likely to be superior to *self*-validation, but it has yet to be developed in most schools.

A third way is to invite a judgment on 'what works' from an independent person, such as an inspector or an expert of some kind. This type of validation is always important: the outsider has an objectivity and disinterestedness denied to even honest and insightful insiders. Pupils are incisive judges of teacher skills and are often in a good position – sometimes more than inspectors – to know whether a teacher's way of teaching is benefiting the quality and extent of their learning, but they are under-used as independent validators.

The capacity of teachers to validate their knowledge is enhanced when the skills of independent outsiders are transferred to them. OfSTED has been a key instrument of both Conservative and Labour government policy for improving quality, and in particular for identifying schools where the level of teacher performance falls below some minimally acceptable standard and so justifies intervention. In this regard, OfSTED has done an important service. Part of the cost, however, has been hostility from many teachers. More important, teachers have not learned, from the process of being inspected, as much as they should and could about how to evaluate themselves. An urgent task for OfSTED is to transfer the skills of inspecting to those who are inspected, so that schools can engage more successfully in self-evaluation and engage in the critically important activity of striving for better practice *with an enhanced capacity to validate their new practices, at the individual teacher and school levels.*

There is a fourth type of validation, namely that provided by educational researchers applying scientific methods to the identification of what works in classrooms. Surely, one might ask, is not this the best source of validation, since researchers are independent yet they use the methods of the social sciences to eliminate the biases and flaws inherent in the other validations? On this view, a central task of educational research is to assist the management of knowledge creation, by:

- identifying a set of core practices relating to teacher effectiveness
- investigating which of these classroom practices work better than others
- specifying the conditions under which the practices are most and least effective
- clarifying the kinds of modification that are needed for teachers to adapt the practices to particular circumstances
- testing the mechanisms by which such practices are disseminated, including the kind of training and support needed for their successful adoption and implementation.

Most teachers believe that there are practices that can potentially be shared within the profession once they have been shown to work. Every teacher and every school should not have to reinvent every educational wheel, but the successful application of what has been discovered elsewhere will always require a sophisticated judgment about their appropriateness to the situation at hand. (Indeed, this has been one of the professional arguments around the national literacy strategy.) Researchers could provide a powerful evidential base for teachers' classroom practices. The Economic and Social Research Council has embarked on a most ambitious programme of educational research directed precisely at this goal: the establishment of evidence-based teaching and learning to match the advances made by doctors who adopt an evidence-based approach to medical practice.

But educational research of this kind, welcome as it is, will only ever produce part of the answer to how to *improve* the quality of teaching. Rapid knowledge creation entails combining the different forms of validation and wherever possible enskilling teachers so that they feel as comfortable with validating as they are with tinkering.

Dissemination as 'inside out' rather than 'outside in'

Reform that is imposed by governments, national or local – the 'top-down' approach – and new ideas that are developed in a research establishment and then disseminated through the school system – the 'centre-periphery' approach – can work to a strictly limited degree, but fail if they are taken to be the main instrument of educational improvement. The alternative is not a totally 'bottom-up' approach in which the initiative is always left to individual schools and teachers to decide on the nature, extent and pace of change. A better strategy brokers partnerships between those involved in the education service, harnessing the energy and commitment to work along agreed paths. Teachers in schools are the main partner, yet they are suspicious of new partnerships. Schools have a natural immunology and they spontaneously resist invasions from foreign bodies, being especially hypersensitive to the Department for Education and Employment or the Qualifications and Curriculum Authority or OfSTED, whose very names are sufficient to arouse the antibodies in some teachers. Transplanting innovations into a school is as risky as transplanting into our bodies a metal prosthesis or an organ donated by some one else; so the prudent reformer first seeks to reduce to a minimum the risk of rapid rejection.

As already discussed, teachers naturally tinker in much of their professional work, and new practices must be presented to them in an inherently modifiable form. *Adequate time and opportunity for such tinkering by teachers is the most powerful immuno-suppressive.* Many of the reforms in curriculum and assessment of the 1990s have not been presented to teachers in this way, thus provoking resistance, distortion and rejection, and the costs in wasted money and teacher energy have been of breathtaking proportions. More recently, the guidance best received by teachers has been the Qualifications and Curriculum Authority's 'schemes of work' which provide examples of how to structure and improve lessons while allowing scope for teachers to combine them with other resources and to 'tinker'.

Schools already investing in the school-based professional development of teachers are likely to be most open to the outside world, for – as was the case with high tech firms – it is when an organisation really needs knowledge to aid its own growth that it actively looks outside for what it can absorb for its own ends. Smart reformers identify the particular spheres in which teachers are already tinkering, for it is here that creativity is to be found in abundance and resistance is at its lowest. This is where knowledge creation flourishes. When teachers are, through tinkering, creating new knowledge, they are most open to ideas and practices from outside. This is also when they are most eager to offer to others what they know and can do, for teachers believe very firmly that the best and most usable ideas come from other teachers. And in this conviction they are very often right.

Improving schools to raise the standards of teaching and learning thus depends on

- identifying those areas in which schools are already engaging in some form of knowledge creation (though it would probably just be called staff development)

- seeing these as the areas on which to build since such an 'inside out' approach does not generate rejection
- finding ways in which the process of knowledge creation can be given greater recognition and support
- helping schools to complete the 'inside out' approach by disseminating knowledge creation skills and the validated outcomes to other schools, in a horizontal or lateral (not 'top-down') manner through partnerships and networks.

I will explore four themes – school-based teacher training, school-based research and development, 'beacon' schools and networking – as means for expanding the scope and reducing the time-scale of the creation of better professional knowledge for every teacher in the education service.

Knowledge creation through school-based teacher training

Teachers are the key asset of schools. They need to be well trained at the beginning of their careers and provided with high quality professional development in subsequent years. Initial teacher training has been the responsibility of higher education. Until recently, in the one-year postgraduate training courses, student teachers spent some two-thirds of their time in the university or college, and one-third on 'teaching practice' in a school, where the student was under the supervision of practising teachers. A member of the university staff would visit the student two or three times during the school placement.

In 1992 Kenneth Baker, then Secretary of State for Education, reversed the time allocations to one-third in the university and two-thirds in school. The majority of teacher trainers were angry, claiming this would lead to a reduction in the quality of new teachers. Some university staff insisted that teachers in school were not good enough to train the next generation of teachers and in any case should not be distracted from their central task of teaching children.

Before this, the practising teachers who had looked after student teachers during teaching practice had been provided neither with guidance and support on their supervisory role nor with financial recompense. This too changed. Supervising teachers became known as 'mentors' and were provided with training. Money was transferred from universities to schools. Following the suggestion of a radical group of teacher trainers, a scheme known as school-centred initial teacher training (or SCITT) was introduced in 1993. Here the student teacher, now usually called a trainee, was recruited by a consortium of schools, which also held the training grant, and could carry out the training alone or, if they so chose, with the help of a university to which money would be paid for services rendered. SCITT was bitterly resented by the university staff, who hailed it as a de-professionalisation of teachers.

School-based initial teacher training has not been the predicted failure, either in terms of the quality of training provided – most schools have reached high levels of provision in a very short time – or in terms of the satisfaction of the trainees – who show no signs of wanting to reduce time in school for more time in the university. What professional novice willingly exchanges on-the-job training with constant support from a current practitioner for off-the-job lectures and seminars led by a former practitioner? What this reform is doing for the practising teachers serving as mentors is also significant. They are responding positively to their new responsibilities and, particularly in SCITT schemes, report feeling revitalised by their involvement in training. The act of supervision forces them to question their own assumptions and practices, to become experimental in trying different ways of teaching, and to be open to reflection and debate about the core activities of teaching.

When mentors teach trainees, they are forced to struggle with the tasks of transferring their tacit knowledge (socialisation in the Nonaka and Takeuchi model) and of making their tacit knowledge explicit so that mentor and trainee can talk about the relevant knowledge and practice (externalisation). Thus mentors typically claim that the act of supervising the trainee is a powerful stimulus to reflection. Through sharing experience and learning by doing under the supervision of the mentor, the trainee acquires professional knowledge (internalisation). Trainees often import new ideas. When shared with the mentor in a form of internal networking, such ideas from the novice jostle with established ideas in the mentor (combination). On-the-job training leads to on-the-job learning, which in turn leads both mentor and trainee to engage in additional tinkering. The mentors' usual tinkerings are made more salient and systematic. Yet it is no longer individualised tinkering, but a version that springs out of a form of knowledge creation using all four modes of knowledge creation. As many headteachers report, the changes have introduced a culture of professional development into the school. It is, of course, more than that: it is culture of professional knowledge creation. It has not been so recognised for a very simple reason: the creation of professional knowledge in any formal sense has been seen as the province of academics in universities, not teachers in schools.

Knowledge creation through school-based educational research and development

'Researchers research, teachers teach.' This has been the slogan of many researchers in their objection to educational research becoming, like initial teacher training, more school-based. School-based R&D is developing more slowly than school-based initial training. Teachers undertake research only in special circumstances, usually when they are registered for a higher degree in a university, where they often receive some training in research design and research methods to help them carry out a piece of empirical research for a dissertation. Typically teachers complete their degree, return to school and never use their acquired research skills again.

As teachers' tinkerings become more salient and systematic through school-based initial training, and a group (rather than individual) endeavour, and as the number of teachers who have taken higher degrees in education increases, the tinkerings become ever closer to research. When the Teacher Training Agency pioneered school-based research consortia, where schools could receive grants to support teacher-led research, the response from schools was strong and positive. A research grant allowed professional tinkering to become more systematic, more collective *and explicitly managed*, so it is turned into knowledge creation. Tinkering often precedes knowledge creation, for it provides, in the form of both explicit and tacit knowledge, much of the raw material for knowledge creation. Funding teachers to do research has huge potential for transforming the hidden tinkerings of teachers into an explicit system of knowledge creation.

Most of the research consortia were keen to work in partnership with university staff, but the general reaction of universities to the principle of school-based research was hostile. Researchers again felt threatened. Because teacher-led research grows out of their professional tinkerings, it is practical in its focus and relevant to the improvement of teaching and learning. But teachers do have limited experience of research design, the techniques of research and data analysis and interpretation. They need help with knowledge validation and university staff can play an immensely important role here. Is not the sensible way forward for researchers to join teachers at the chalk face, working in partnership to create better professional knowledge of teaching and learning? The teachers have for decades been willing to work on university premises and on terms set by the university. Is there not scope for some reversal in the interests of getting a better balance in the partnership?

In short, university-based teacher trainers and researchers have engaged in a defence of Mode 1, university-centred knowledge production and have argued that the trend to school-based teacher training and research poses a dangerous threat to quality. Their advice to policy-makers has been to restore the *status quo ante.* This is, of course, both misguided and self-serving. The government should not listen: it should recognise that school-based training and research are vital elements in the movement to Mode 2 or applied partnership approach to knowledge production. The task is to get teacher trainers to realise that they are important partners in the Mode 2 creation of better professional knowledge for teachers, but that the nature of their role changes in the common enterprise to enhance classroom skills for better learning by students.

Such changes are painful for researchers, but are they risky? Is there evidence that these changes are successful in knowledge-intensive businesses and industry?

'We don't have a separate R&D laboratory ... the development work is done right here on the manufacturing floor'... R&D ... is heavily decentralised, with 90 to 99 per cent of research and development conducted within small operating groups – close to, or even actually within, their regular manufacturing facilities.... Innovation cannot be walled off as the responsibility of a small clearly defined group for formally designated innovators. Rather, innovation must pervade the firm, with roots and links in all key functional areas ... Stage barriers – between research and development, between development and manufacturing – must be transcended and integrated ... Overlap, contact and negotiation are the norms. (Jelinek & Schoonhoven, 1990)

This incorporation [of scientific knowledge into production] depends not only on the transfer of researchers to development and production, but also on initial immigration of development and production engineers to inventional activities. Similarly, extracorporate professors, researchers and engineers may be interlinked (and sometimes imported) from the same sort of sources to the project. (Harryson, 1998)

Bringing together a research community and a practitioner community in joint action closes the gap between them. If this happens in successful industries, would there not be benefits if some educational researchers migrated to schools and more teachers were seconded into higher education? That high tech engineers take such radical steps to close the gap between researchers and users offers a useful lesson. Educational researchers and users are in different locations, making intensive interaction difficult to achieve, and each side starts from a very different knowledge base. Sometimes this difference is of little consequence, but where the focus of professional knowledge creation is teaching and learning, the knowledge gap between researcher and practitioner is big enough to make the researcher-led creation of knowledge distinctly hazardous. Knowledge creation is heavily concerned with the mobilisation of the tacit knowledge of the active professional, but many researchers simply do not share the tacit knowledge of teachers, because either they have never been schoolteachers or it is some years since they were. The tacit knowledge in the researcher's knowledge base is quite unlike that of the practising teacher. Moreover, researchers often lack the specific, local knowledge of the schools and classrooms and of the teachers and students involved in the research. In high technology firms, this grasp of local knowledge plays a vital role in knowledge creation.

As things stand, it is difficult for researchers and teachers to find an arena in which they can negotiate the agenda for research on teaching and learning. Teachers are in danger of being the passive objects of research rather than active partners who contribute to the creation and dissemination of new knowledge. The *status quo* in educational research hinders the creation of knowledge to improve teaching and learning. In school-based initial teacher training and school-based research, a fundamental reconstruction of relations between schools and universities has been initiated. If knowledge creation through school-based training and R&D become ever more natural parts of a teacher's work, this could be a powerful incentive to recruit more able graduates into the profession. The public image of the teacher is of a person who is *coping* not *creating*. To improve the image of teaching and the intellectual quality of its intake there must be more opportunities in school for all teachers to engage in creative work that is intellectually stretching and professionally satisfying.

Knowledge validation will gain greater sophistication in schools where teachers who have done research for a higher degree have opportunities to apply investigative skills to their practices. But is the social scientific validation of professional knowledge by formal research always the best form of validation? There is no simple answer, but I suggest that once teachers have gained confidence in knowledge creation, they will explore new forms of knowledge validation.

There are professional groups, apart from researchers in social science, who might be a source of ideas for this. In courts of law, evidence is any material which tends to persuade the court of the truth or probability of some asserted claim. Courts conform to 'rules of evidence' developed over the years. Among educators, evidence of the effectiveness of a practice and its underlying knowledge might be regarded as any material which persuades practitioners of the effectiveness of the practice under examination. Just as in law courts rules of evidence have evolved about the admissibility of certain kinds of evidence, the weight of evidence and the standard of proof, so educational practitioners might develop rules of evidence to apply to their own circumstances. Knowledge-creating teachers do not have to rely entirely on the social science of educational researchers for knowledge validation; rather they can treat new methods validating their knowledge as a potential outcome of their own knowledge creation.

Knowledge creation through beacon schools

The idea behind the government's 'beacon' schools is simple. OfSTED, through inspection, identifies outstanding schools which may then bid for money to support the dissemination of their 'good practices' to other schools. No one knows whether this will work. It is an act of ministerial faith. Some teachers see it as a nasty, elitist strategy: shakily based on OfSTED nominations, schools are divided into 'beacon' and 'just ordinary' schools. More important, this could be yet another version of the discredited linear model: one kind of school has some important knowledge; this is passed to other schools who are thought to need it; the recipients are then supposed to implement what they are told or see.

So will the beacon school experiment work?

The dissemination of professional knowledge and skill takes two forms. Knowledge has to be disseminated from one person to another; we might call this 'knowledge transfer'. In a second form, the knowledge is disseminated from one place (a classroom, a school) to another; we might call this 'knowledge transposition'.

The transfer of practical knowledge between professionals involves far more than telling or simply providing information. If one teacher tells another about a practice that the first finds effective, the second teacher has merely acquired information, not personal knowledge. Transfer occurs only when the knowledge of the first teacher becomes information for the second, who then works on that information in such a way that it becomes part of his or her context of meaning and purpose and pre-existing knowledge and then is applied in action. Teachers differ in their beliefs, values and ways of working. Transfer is the conversion of information about one person's practice into another's know-how. It is a very complex piece of interpersonal engineering or transplantation – which explains why so much dissemination falters and fails after the initial steps. Dissemination makes the information more widely available, but does not provide the support

Figure 3. A model of dissemination of good practice

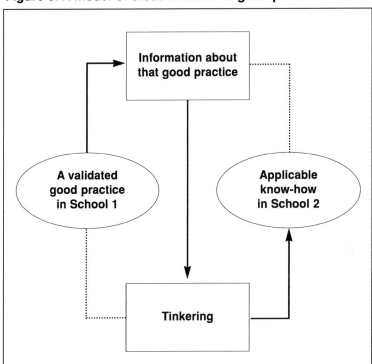

which allows the receiver of the information to convert it into personal knowledge that can be successfully applied.

The missing element, of course, is the tinkering. Conversion of *abstract information into applicable know-how* is the very essence of transfer and it makes sense that it is most easily achieved when a teacher tinkers with information about a 'good practice' and tests it and, where necessary, modifies it to fit a different context and, on finding that it works, then adopts it (see Figure 3). When two or more teachers can tinker together, the transfer of knowledge between them is most likely to succeed; and when there is little opportunity for joint tinkering, the lone tinkerer is more likely to lose faith or interest in the new practice, and so gives up and the attempted transfer fails. It is this vital element of supported joint tinkering that well-intentioned disseminators usually overlook. Joint tinkering is in reality is a form of knowledge creation, and so is more likely to work than a crude, linear version of dissemination.

Teachers tinkering together will enjoy a successful partnership if they believe they all have something to gain from the collaboration. A beacon school where staff are effective, but complacent about their skills, will not make a good job of dissemination. An effective school that sees itself as a learning organisation committed to continual improvement will make the best beacon school, for it will look to its partners as yet another resource for enhancing the professional knowledge of its staff still further. It will see the beacon school initiative as involving a two-way process of transfer and transposition, and so develop a philosophy of 'mutual growth' rather than an attitude of 'come-and-see-how-well-we-are-doing-and-you-might-learn-something-useful'. As with high tech firms, no single school has the answer to all the emerging problems, so both can work as equal partners in the creation of some new knowledge to their mutual benefit.

The first cohort of beacons – others will be named later – should be a test-bed for the discovery of the knowledge underlying the successful transfer and transposition of effective teaching and learning. Beacon schools may be more effective schools than average, but there is no reason for believing that they have particular skills or experience in disseminating their professional practices. Yet it is on just such knowledge that their success as beacon schools rests. So they will have to *create* this knowledge. Government policy, that effective practice should be disseminated from a minority of effective schools to the rest in a short time scale, depends on the creation of professional knowledge on effective dissemination. The beacon school experiment, like that of the Education Action Zones, provides the opportunity for this.

Knowledge creation through networking

Confining the creation of professional knowledge to the idiosyncratic tinkerings of individual teachers, or to a limited number of beacon schools and their partners, does far too little to improve teaching and learning. A more deliberate, explicit and collective process of professional knowledge creation depends on inventing new forms of networking. *Internal networking* among functional and cross-functional teams remains under-developed in most schools and, in contrast to the organisation of successful electronics firms, schools are hierarchical and compartmentalised. When a group of schools, either in a local or 'virtual' consortium, works on the same topic of professional knowledge creation and validation through a process of *external networking*, national progress in advancing the quality of teaching and learning could be rapid and cumulative. The new information and communication technologies play a major role in networking for professional knowledge creation, shared tinkering and concurrent dissemination. They do so on a scale and at a rate that has hitherto been almost unimaginable, and so justify government investment in them. For secondary schools, they also support the emergence of subject-specialist knowledge creation networks, ending the isolation of teachers specialising in a particular subject of the curriculum, when there are often just one or two such teachers in a single school. Networks are particularly valuable to very small or isolated schools whose staff need to tap into the experience and knowledge of teachers located elsewhere.

Networks de-privatise the classroom and so are the key to this different model of dissemination in which *all* schools can now be linked through ICT and so *all* can take part in the activities of professional knowledge creation, application and dissemination. Again, the business world provides a model for education. In industries where the knowledge is both complex and expanding and the sources of expertise are widely dispersed – as is becoming the case in education – the locus of innovation is to be found in networks of learning. Innovating companies:

are executing nearly every step in the production process, from discovery to distribution, through some form of external collaboration. These various forms of inter-firm alliance take on many forms ... The R&D intensity or level of technological sophistication of industries is positively correlated with the intensity and number of alliances ... Knowledge creation occurs in the context of a community ... To stay current in a rapidly moving field requires that an organisation has a hand in the research process. Passive recipients of new knowledge are less likely to appreciate its value or to be able to respond rapidly. In industries in which know-how is critical, companies must be expert at both in-house research and cooperative research with such external partners as university scientists ... A firm's value and ability as a collaborator is related to its internal assets, but at the same time collaboration further develops and strengthens those internal competencies ... When the locus of innovation is found in an inter-organisational network, access to that network proves critical. R&D alliances are the admission ticket, the foundation for more diverse types of collaboration and the pivot around which firms become more centrally connected.... As a result of this reciprocal learning, both *firm-level* and *industry-level* practices are evolving. (Powell, Koput & Smith-Doerr, 1996, italics added)

At first sight, this picture is surprising, for don't we expect high tech firms, where commercial success depends on the creation and rapid utilisation of new knowledge, to develop ruthlessly competitive relationships in which new knowledge is closely guarded? The reality is that though they undoubtedly need to keep some secrets, they know that knowledge is advancing at such a rate that no single firm, however large, can expect to know everything that is potentially needed. It is therefore in their common interest that there should be considerable sharing of knowledge through networking. Sharing is not incompatible with self-interest.

Here is a vision – one that shatters the stereotype of how things work in industry – of how networks within and between schools could promote professional knowledge creation within the individual school *and in the education service as a whole*. The result is a knowledge-creating school system, a web of interlinked knowledge-creating schools. Networks are crucial to the high levels of communication and exchange on which knowledge creation, dissemination and use so heavily depend.

> The ... firm, then, takes on some of the characteristics of a
> spider's web. Each node is a problem-solving team pos-
> sessing a unique combination of skills. It is linked to
> other nodes by a potentially large number of lines of com-
> munication. To survive each firm must be permeable to
> new types of knowledge and *the sector as a whole*
> becomes increasingly interconnected. The interconnec-
> tions embrace not only other firms but many other knowl-
> edge producing groups, be they in government research
> laboratories, research institutes, consultancies or universi-
> ties ... This new infrastructure depends upon innovation in
> the telecommunications and computer industries that will
> make possible the ever closer interaction of an increasing
> number of knowledge centres. (Gibbons *et al*, 1994, ital-
> ics added)

Teachers' peers are the most credible source of new knowledge and how to apply it. For teachers, access to *know-how* depends heavily on their knowledge of *know-who*, and it is time to capitalise on the fact. Networking through ICT maximises the *know-who* at the heart of rapid dissemination.

'Networks,' says Manuel Castells (1996), 'constitute the new social morphology of our societies, and the diffusion of networking logic substantially modifies the operation and outcomes of processes of production, experience, power and culture.' As teachers start to network with other teachers and schools, they will deploy these same networking skills to communicate and interact with other communities – parents, employers, groups in the locality and any other partners who have a potential contribution to make to the quality of school life. And in so doing they will become good role models for students entering the network society.

Policies for the new partnerships

A key to the transition to Mode 2 or applied partnerships is the inclusion of teachers in schools in the construction of the research agenda and the execution of research projects. Yet they are denied the opportunity to engage in research, since they lack necessary time and funding. Policies will have to be devised, building on the pioneering work of the Teacher Training Agency, to fund schools to release teachers for research and professional knowledge creation. Action at national level could create the necessary infrastructure in addition to the funding. Each region or local education authority could create a cadre of teachers with some research training, obtained as part of a higher degree in education, to work on topics for knowledge creation assigned a high priority by local schools. Teacher-researchers could be involved in part-time research, say one to two days a week, or occasionally full-time where a project is particularly ambitious or urgent. University staff play a key role here, especially as consultants in the design of teacher-led research, in the coordination of multisite projects, and where appropriate in developing the theoretical base for research. The relationship between research, knowledge creation and practice could be an important area for work for the proposed National Leadership College for headteachers.

The universities should now take a powerful role in initiating, supporting and coordinating *networks and webs for educational research and professional knowledge creation* which would range from small-scale knowledge creation in a consortium of two or three schools to large-scale multi-site experiments when emergent knowledge requires sophisticated validation. If the universities do not undertake these functions, it is difficult to see how Mode 2 educational research will be a success.

It is only when much more practical and applicable professional knowledge about effective teaching and learning is created that the significantly higher standards of education can be achieved in the nation's schools. The process of knowledge creation is the key to the education service's long-term capacity to rise continuously to the challenges and opportunities of the knowledge society, most of which cannot at present be foreseen and planned for.

The expansion of Mode 2 knowledge creation will not take place without government intervention. Advocacy of the knowledge-creating school as a path to more effective schools and to better educational research should not be confused with a 1960s-style policy of 'letting a thousand flowers bloom' in the education service. Knowledge creation, with its emphasis on knowledge validation, eschews a 'do-as-you-please' philosophy and insists on a tightly focused and disciplined framework for developing and diffusing high quality professional practices. The creation of such a framework is the responsibility of the government, in association with all the partners – the Economic and Social Research Council, the Higher Education Funding Councils, the Teacher Training Agency, the LEAs, the researchers and, most important of all, the teachers.

> The appearance of Mode 2 is creating new challenges for government. National institutions need to be de-centred – to be made more permeable – and governments through their policies can promote change in this direction. These policies will become more effective if, concurrently, they become more proactive brokers in a knowledge production game. (Gibbons et al, 1994)

Testimony from the knowledge-creating school

In knowledge-creating schools, the experiences of teaching and learning will be different for all involved. There will be many drivers towards the learning organisations of the emerging knowledge society, some of which at present look marginal and so are overlooked and others which cannot yet be seen. In these early stages, government plays a key role in shaping the educational future by setting national standards and providing the infrastructure and support for the other key player – the teachers – whose work in improving and creating their professional knowledge at the local level can, through networks, become a national achievement in support of national objectives. The teachers will have to choose to shape their future, which will require courage and imagination, virtues in ample supply among the profession, which have been drawn upon too rarely recent years. The opportunity for both government and teachers is there to be grasped.

A teacher
When I joined the staff it was a shock to discover that you have to give up time to work on two task groups. You never know who you're going to have to work with next, so people make an effort to avoid the conflict and petty quarrels that spoil so many staff rooms.

A mathematics teacher
I'm finding that my class is making progress since we started the course on 'thinking skills'. We're part of a multi-site trial that's being coordinated by the School of Education in the local university and we hope soon to publish the results of the trials on the DfEE database and exchange views with other teachers in the DfEE's virtual teachers' centre.

A headteacher
I spend quite a bit of time out of school, talking with our partners and keeping an eye open for any new idea or opportunity that we

must use to help us with our mission. At the moment, I'm negotiating with a group who want to use our ICT facilities to increase their chances of work. They want to come and do it when the students are not here. I'm trying to persuade them to do some of it when the students are here, because I know it benefits both sides.

A geography teacher
I'm on several task groups that work across the subject departments. My favourite one at the moment is the team that's testing our independent homework assignments in which parents help students by using some of the latest parent-friendly materials now becoming available through digital television services. Not all the students have access to these at home, so they work together in the homes of those that do. To achieve this, we've linked in with another task group that's already made some progress with developing a peer tutoring scheme.

A deputy head
We're a beacon school, and have two partner schools. We're sharing some of our best practices with them, and they're doing an internal investigation to check what they think their best practices are. We're then going to try to validate them and see what can be transposed to our school. We use the latest ICT so we can watch their lessons from here. Not having to go to their school every time we want to see something saves so much time.

A student
I'm in year 11 and I enjoy the new system of coming to school on only one Friday in three. Instead, we work at home or in the computer room on our own or in a group. On the Fridays I have to be in school, I get a half hour individual tutorial link in university. It's good: the teacher really helps me.

A head of department
I've just become a mentor to one of our trainee teachers and I've been surprised how much I'm enjoying it. The best bit is when we

realise that something that we're doing in the classroom is not really working, so we put our heads together and think out something better. Then we take it in turns to see if we can make it work in practice. And sometimes it does!

A student

I'm a student and I'm a member of a research project that's finding out what people think of school reports and how we can improve them. We've been checking out what students and their parents think are the strengths and weaknesses of the format of the termly report to parents. We've had some help from a researcher in the university and I find all my research skills that I need in other subjects are getting better through this work.

A parent

I've recently joined a class for adults to develop my IT skills. It should help with my job and it certainly helps me keep up with helping my children. As a matter of fact, my own son is one of the 'teachers'. It's wonderful to find yourself being taught by your own son and the exercise is really boosting his self-confidence.

Head of business studies

We've been having two people from the financial services industry doing some part-time teaching in the school and acting as mentors to some of the less motivated students. They want to learn from us because they eventually get our students and have to train them further. We get a feel of how they act towards our students. The whole thing links what we're doing here to the real world.

A teacher

I'm acting as the school's research coordinator this year, partly because I'm doing a Master's degree at the university so I have some obvious contacts when they're needed. We always have several projects on the go and I act as the link person and as a general resource. I plan to build my dissertation around this work.

Museum education officer

I'm working with the school on a project on the industrial revolution. It's linked into the GCSE. We're planning to bring another partner from industry and then make a link with the careers service. We're being very ambitious, I know, but it makes the work the students are doing so much more real and relevant. We're gaining confidence about partnerships and networks through all this.

Sources and suggestions for reading

Alexander R, 1992, *Policy and Practice in Primary Education*, Routledge, London.

Bentley T, 1998, *Learning Beyond the Classroom: Education for a changing world*, Routledge, London.

Castells M, 1996, *The Rise of the Network Society*, Blackwell, Oxford.

Drucker P F, 1993, *Post-Capitalist Society*, Butterworth-Heinemann, Oxford.

Gibbons M, Limoges C, Nowotny H, Schwatzman S, Scott P and Trow M, 1994, *The New Production of Knowledge*, Sage, London.

Handy C, 1989, *The Age of Unreason*, Hutchinson Business, London.

Harryson S, 1998, *Japanese Technology and Innovation Management*, Edward Elgar, Cheltenham.

Huberman M, 1992, 'Teacher development and instructional mastery' in Hargreaves A and Fullan MG, eds, *Understanding Teacher Development*, Cassell, London.

Jelinek M and Schoonhoven CB, 1990, *The Innovation Marathon*, Blackwell, Oxford.

Leadbeater C and Goss S, 1998, *Civic Entrepreneurship*, Demos, London.

Leonard-Barton D, 1995, *Wellsprings of Knowledge*, Harvard Business School Press, Cambridge, Massachusetts.

Nelson RR, 1996, 'National innovation systems: a retrospective on a study' in Dosi G and Malerba F, eds, *Organisation and Strategy in the Evolution of the Enterprise*, Macmillan, London.

Nonaka I and Takeuchi H, 1995, *The Knowledge-Creating Company*, Oxford University Press, Oxford.

Powell WW, Koput KW and Smith-Doerr L, 1996, 'Inter-organisational collaboration and the locus of innovation: networks of learning in biotechnology', *Administrative Science Quarterly*, no 41, 116-145.

Roos RJ, Dragonette NC and Edvinsson L, 1997, *Intellectual Capital: Navigating the new business landscape*, Macmillan, London.

Sammons P, Hillman J and Mortimore P, 1995, *Key Characteristics of Effective Schools*, University of London Institute of Education/Office for Standards in Education, London.